Pentagram

LAURENCE KING

Published in 2010 by Laurence King Publishing Ltd
361–373 City Road
London EC1V 1LR
United Kingdom
Tel: +44 20 7841 6900
Fax: +44 20 7841 6910
e-mail: enquiries@laurenceking.com
www.laurenceking.com

A catalogue record for this book is available
from the British Library

ISBN: 978-1-85669-668-5

Printed in China

Pentagram: Marks
400 Symbols and Logotypes

Laurence King Publishing

Founded in 1972 by an architect, an industrial designer, and three graphic designers, the international design consultancy Pentagram has been interdisciplinary from the start. But central to its practice is the question of identity. How can the tools of design be used to help a client express its unique character, whether through a building, a product, or a piece of communication?

The answer, at its most concise, can be found in this book. The four hundred marks reproduced within these pages represent the diverse array of identity work created by Pentagram partners, past and present. Over the past four decades, the firm has designed marks for large corporations and small businesses, government agencies and non-profit institutions, clubs, societies, and even individuals. Each of them sought a representative symbol to appear on business cards, brochures, books, products, buildings, websites, wherever the institution meets the public eye.

The solution to this problem can take many forms, and shown here are examples of every possibility: typographic wordmarks, pictorial symbols, abstract marks. Isolating them in black and white helps us appreciate these marks as unique formal solutions, and highlights the contrasts and occasional similarities among them. But this presentation is also somewhat deceptive, for a logo is rarely a solitary commission. Rather, produced in conjunction with a unified graphics, architecture or product design program, at its best it represents the starting point for a much larger effort.

The practice of design has changed radically since the seventies, but its concerns have remained remarkably constant. The seemingly simple graphic exercise of designing a mark for a client — and the elusive quest for timelessness that this exercise almost inevitably entails — is a fascinating metaphor for the challenges that designers have always faced, and will continue to face as we move further into a new century.

Academy of Achievement 1991
Not-for-profit foundation that puts young people
in contact with America's achievers

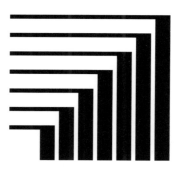

Aga Khan Fund for Economic Development 1986
Charitable foundation

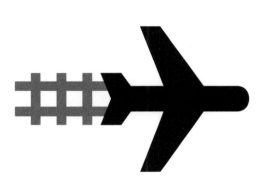

AirTrain 1998
Light rail system that links New York's airports
to its mass transit systems

Alibris 1998
Supplier of rare, used and hard-to-find books

Alliance for a Healthier Generation 2006
Joint venture of the William J. Clinton Foundation
and the American Heart Association established to
combat childhood obesity

Almaty Financial District 2007
International financial centre in
Almaty, Kazakhstan

Amanda Wakeley 2000
London couture designer

Ambigram 2008
Greek advertising agency

American Folk Art Museum 2000
Museum of traditional American folk art and crafts

HQRSE

American Quarter Horse Association 2001
Quarter Horse breed registry and
membership organisation

ANNA

Anna Pugh 1962
Logotype for an illustrator

ArcSight

ArcSight 2001
Security management for corporate
computer networks

Art and Architecture 1991
Society promoting collaboration between
artists and architects

ArtCenter

Art Center College of Design 1988
Art and design school in Pasadena, California

ART
INSTITVTE
CHICAGO

Art Institute of Chicago 2008
World-renowned art museum founded in 1879

Arts Council of Great Britain 1997
Symbol endorsing the Arts Council's lottery
funded endowments

ARUP

Arup 1985
International civil engineering consultancy

Asea Brown Boveri 1987
Multinational engineering company with operations
in over 100 countries

Asia Society 1987
Dedicated to fostering an understanding of and
communication between Americans and the
peoples of the Asia-Pacific region

Asprey

Asprey 2002
Quintessentially British luxury goods brand
founded in 1781

The Atheneum 1990
Luxury hotel in the Greektown area of Detroit

the Atlantic

The Atlantic 2008
One of America's oldest monthly magazines

B2B Equality 2000
Electronic information exchange for start-up
companies and entrepreneurs

Bach 2000
Festival of classical music by the German composer

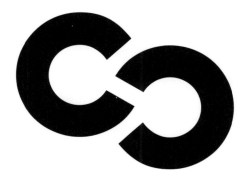

**Bard College Center for Curatorial Studies
and Art in Contemporary Culture** 1992
Exhibition and research facility dedicated to the study
of art and curatorial practices

**Bard Graduate Center for Studies in the
Decorative Arts, Design, and Culture** 1993
Manhattan-based institution dedicated to the study
of the applied arts

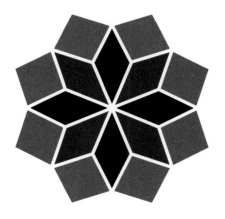

BASE-MK 2007
Real estate development firm

Battersea Pie Station 2008
Cafés specialising in classic London pie and mash

B|D|N|A

BDNA 2008
IT asset management company

Beacon 1999
Manhattan restaurant built around a huge,
hearth-like wood-burning oven

THE BERKELEY

The Berkeley 1995
Luxurious hotel in London's Knightsbridge

Bertazzoni 2005
Family-owned Italian manufacturer of
professional-style cooking ranges

Better Work 2008
Foundation dedicated to improving labour
standards in global supply chains

Biba 1963
Iconic sixties fashion boutique

BitStreams 2002
Exhibition of digital artwork held at the
Whitney Museum of American Art

Black & White Ball 2008
Fundraising event for the San Francisco Symphony

Black Box Theater 2008
Theatre at the Maryland Institute College
of Art, Baltimore

Brandspanking 2007
Producers of branded media content

Breaking the Ice 2005
International not-for-profit organisation that seeks to
transform conflicts into trust and mutual respect

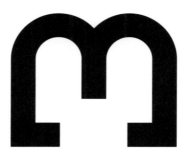

Bridges 2007
Capital campaign for the Judah L. Magnes Museum
of Jewish Culture

Brill's Content 2000
Magazine of investigative journalism focused
on the media

Broadway Books 1995
Division of Bantam Doubleday Dell named for the
thoroughfare that bisects Manhattan's street grid

Brooklyn Academy of Music 1995
Venue for avant-garde performing arts

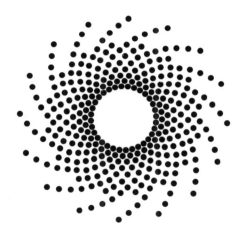

Brooklyn Historical Society 2005
Institution dedicated to the appreciation
of New York's most populous borough

BRUNSWICK

Brunswick 2004
Corporate communications advisors

Buddakan 1998
Chic Philadelphia restaurant serving
pan-Asian cuisine

Building One at Atlantic Yards 2008
Proposed Frank Gehry-designed building
in Brooklyn, New York

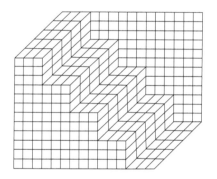

Buro Happold 1977
International structural engineering firm

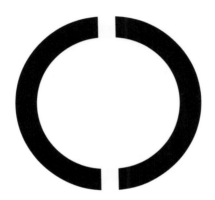

CaliDerma 2007
Pharmaceutical-grade line of skincare products

California Academy of Sciences 2007
Science institution housing a museum, planetarium
and aquarium

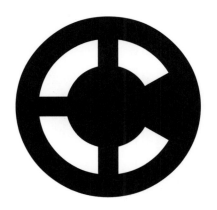

Callaway Golf 2000
Manufacturer of golfing equipment

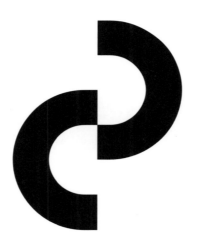

Capital Partners 2006
International real estate development firm

Cass Art 2003
London-based chain of art supply stores

Celebration, Florida 1993
New Urbanist community near Orlando, Florida

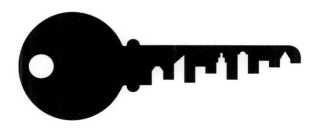

Center for Architecture 2001
Public centre dedicated to New York and the
built environment

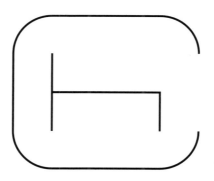

Chambers Hotel 2001
Boutique hotel in midtown Manhattan with
a downtown aesthetic

FIFTEEN CIRCULAR

Circular 2007
Magazine of the Typographic Circle, a typography
association based in the UK

Citi 2000
The world's largest financial institution

Claridge's

Claridge's 1995
Historic five-star London society hotel

Classical.com 2001
Online classical music retailer

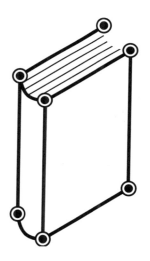

Classmap 2000
Online class notes, curriculum and schedules

CloudShield 2001
Computer network security company

c|net

CNET 1993
Internet and television-based technology
information network

The **co-operative**

The Co-operative 2005
The world's largest consumer-owned retailer

Columbia Business School 2007
Graduate school of business at Columbia University

COLUMBUS

Columbus Foods 2007
Manufacturer and purveyor of salame
and premium meats

Columbus Regional Hospital 1991
Indiana healthcare centre

Commercial Bank of Kuwait 1980
Consumer and corporate bank founded in 1960

Connecting Congress 2006
Design conference co-sponsored by the International
Council of Societies of Industrial Design and the
Industrial Designers Society of America

CONTEMPORARY JEWISH MUSEUM

Contemporary Jewish Museum 2007
San Francisco museum that explores contemporary
perspectives on Jewish culture, history, art and ideas

Coram 2000
The UK's oldest children's charity

Corella Publishing 2006
Producer of illustrated books and documentaries

Cornell Lab of Ornithology 2008
Identity based on the work of wildlife artist Charley
Harper for an institute whose mission is to interpret
and conserve the earth's biodiversity

Council of Fashion Designers of America 1992
Not-for-profit trade association for designers of
fashion and fashion accessories

Courts at Birch Meadows 2002
Tennis club in Greenwich, Connecticut

Crafts Council 1991
UK national development agency for
contemporary crafts

The Criterion Collection 2006
Publishers of classic and contemporary
cinema on DVD

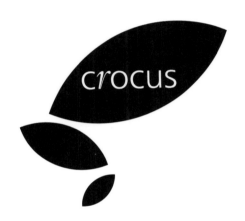

Crocus 2000
Online garden centre

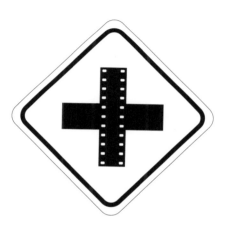

Crossroads Films 1989
Film production company

Cruel World 1999
Employment referral service

curiouspictures

Curious Pictures 1993
Mixed media, live action, animation and computer
graphics studio

D&AD 1962
International association that represents the
creative, design and advertising industries

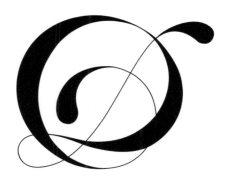

Dallas Opera 1978
Performing arts company

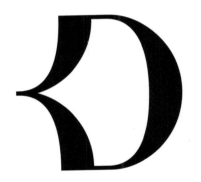

Damiani 2001
Luxury jewellery brand based in Milan

Dana Centre 2003
Forum for education and debate at the
London Science Museum

Dehesa Gago 2000
Fine Spanish wine produced by Telmo Rodriguez

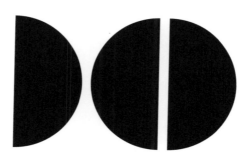

Design Objectives 1972
Manufacturing and marketing company

Delta Faucet Company 2001
Manufacturer of domestic and commercial faucets

Design Within Reach 2000
Retailer of contemporary furniture

Detroit Institute of Arts 2006

Fine arts museum founded in 1885

Detroit Symphony Orchestra 2001
Performing arts organisation and landmark
orchestra hall

Dick Bruna Huis 2005
Permanent collection housed at the Centraal
Museum in Utrecht, celebrating the work of
the creator of "Miffy"

Digital DNA 1998
An "ingredient brand" of Motorola

DMAT - SDMI 1999
International consortium of digital music and
technology companies

The Dorchester

The Dorchester 2003
Luxury hotel on Park Lane, London

Dorchester Collection 2006
Worldwide portfolio of five-star hotels

Dorling Kindersley 2003
Updated identity for an international publisher
of illustrated reference books

Dragoncloud 2001
Range of premium organic teas

East Coast Greenway 2005
3,000-mile traffic-free path linking cities from
Maine to Florida

EAT.

Eclipse 2006
Lost, forgotten or overshadowed film classics
from The Criterion Collection

Editions de l'Olivier 1991
French publishing house

Editions Payot 1988
French publishing house

1837

1837 1998
Restaurant at Brown's Hotel in Mayfair, London

180K

1801 K Street 2007
Office building in Washington, D.C.

Electra 2000
European private equity investors

Elektra Entertainment 1989
American record label

Emerald City Press 2007
Coffee, news and flower shop in Austin, Texas

En Garde Arts 1997
Not-for-profit avant-garde theatre group based
in New York City

Equazen 1997
Makers of dietary supplements

ESPA

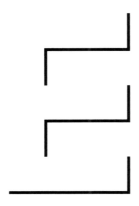

Essenziale 2007
Lingerie and swimwear boutique in Mayfair, London

ESTĒE LAUDER

Estée Lauder 1994
Manufacturer and marketer of skincare, makeup,
fragrance and haircare products

Eureka! 1987
Children's museum

Eva 1981
Lithographic printer

Fast Ed 1999
Software training company

Faber & Faber 1981
Independent literary publishing house

Faber Music 1981
Sheet music division of Faber & Faber

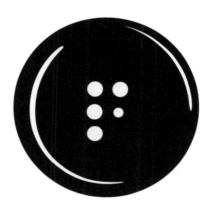

The Fashion Center 1996
Business improvement district encouraging the
development of New York's Garment District

FASHION FRINGE

Fashion Fringe 2006
Finding and supporting the next generation
of British fashion designers

Fast Take 1999
Interactive kiosks for US video rental stores

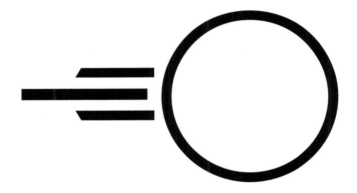

Fastball 2007
Rock band from Austin, Texas

Fine Line Features 1991
Film production company

Finest★

Tesco Finest 1998
Premium range of food and drink for Tesco

Fireside 1999
Imprint of Simon & Schuster publishing games
and self-improvement titles

Five Franklin Place 2008
Condominium residences in New York

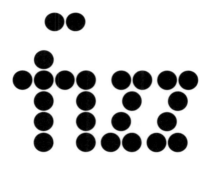

Fizz 2001
Healthcare marketing company

Flatiron/23rd Street Partnership 2007
Business improvement district in New York
surrounding the intersection of Fifth Avenue,
23rd Street and Broadway

Folio:

Folio 2001
Publishing industry news magazine

450 Park Avenue 2007
Iconic black granite office tower in Manhattan

Fox River Paper 1988
American paper manufacturer

frankfurt

Frankfurt 2004
City of Frankfurt, Germany

The Friends of Normand Park 2008
Association for the redevelopment of a public
park in south-west London

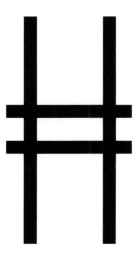

Friends of the High Line 2005
Advocating the preservation of the elevated railway
on Manhattan's West Side

Galleria Colonna 1990
Italian shopping and business centre

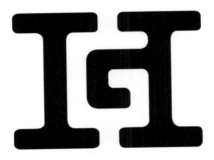

Gebrüder Heinemann 1975
Distribution, logistics and a chain of retail stores
for the international travel industry

Geronimo Inns 2003
Gastropubs in London and the south-east
of England

gettyimages

Getty Images 2000
Stock photography library

The Glass House 2007
Philip Johnson's iconic residence in New Canaan,
Connecticut, now part of the National Trust for
Historic Preservation

GOLLA 2007
Producer of high-resolution transmission
electron microscopes

The Good Diner 1992
Traditional American diner in New York City

Good Guys 1999
Retailer of high-quality PC and electronics merchandise

Goods & Chattels 1960s
UK importer of household items

Gotham Equities 1992
New York real estate development firm

Granary Associates 1995
Philadelphia-based architecture and
engineering firm

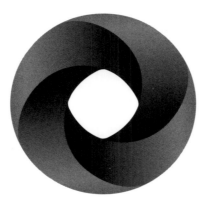

GraficEurope 2003
Annual pan-European graphic design conference

Green Canteen 2008
Brooklyn restaurant that offers locally sourced and
environmentally friendly dishes

The **Guardian**

The Guardian 1988
UK national newspaper

GYMBOREE

Gymboree 1995
Manufacturer and retailer of children's products

Hafen Offenbach 2006
Property development project
in Offenbach, Germany

Halfords 2001
Retailer of bicycles, car care products, parts
and accessories

HEAL'S

Heal's 2005
Retailers of contemporary furniture and homeware

Heart Center 1979
Clinic for cardiological disorders

Hemasafe 1995
Autologous blood bank franchise

HEMISPHERES

Hemispheres 1992
United Airlines in-flight magazine

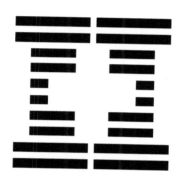

Hermann Hospital 1989
Part of the Texas Medical Center in Houston

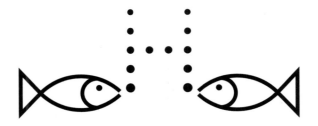

Higgins Retreat 2003
Seaside retreat and conference for the
Higgins Group

Hotel Hankyu International 1996
Luxury flagship hotel in Osaka, Japan

HSK 2006
Group of hospitals in the Rhein-Main region
of Germany

Hulton|Archive

Hulton Archive 2000
Getty Images' collection of historic
editorial photography

I Teach NYC 2008
Recruitment initiative for the New York City
Department of Education

IDEO 1997
Identity for the Palo Alto-based product
development firm updated from the
Paul Rand original

iHelp 2000
Travellers' information service for New York's airports

Il Sole 24 ORE 1979
Italian business and financial newspaper

ila 2007
Organic skincare and well-being products

INDIVIDUAL
SOLUTIONS

Individual Solutions 2006
Car fitter specialising in the customisation
of off-road vehicles

Ingram Partnership 2003
Media strategy consultants

Institute of Directors 1993
International business association
for company directors

Interactive Week 2000
Newspaper for the web development industry

Internet Advertising Bureau 2008
Trade association for online advertising

Is Molas 2006
Golf course and hotel on the island of Sardinia

The Island 2000
Pay-as-you-go airport lounges for BAA

IZOD

IZOD 1997
Sports and casual clothing brand

Jamaica Station 1998
Multi-modal railway station in New York featuring
a large curved roof

Jazz at Lincoln Center 2004
New York institution for the performance, teaching
and recording of jazz

Jo's Jewellery 2005
Independent jewellery designer

John Lewis

John Lewis 2002
Chain of department stores

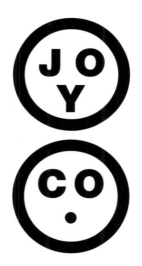

Joyco 1999
International confectionery group based in Spain

Kagan

Kagan 2001
Provider of media and communications industry
business intelligence

Kanuhura 2004
Luxury island resort in the Maldives

Kaufman Center 2002
Concert hall and musical arts school in Manhattan

King's College London 1992
Prestigious educational institution, part of the
University of London

Krautheim Concepts 2003
Classical musicians' agent

Kubota 1989
Machinery manufacturer based in Osaka, Japan

L.L.Bean

L.L. Bean 2008
American apparel and outdoor equipment retailer for
more than 95 years

Lands' End 2003
Direct merchant of classic American apparel

Las Vegas Magazine 2007
Weekly city magazine

Launchpad 2008
Interactive gallery for children in London's
Science Museum

Lead Development Association 1970s
Conference on electric powered vehicles

LeoLogic 1998
French software development company

Lifemark 1999
Providing services to chronically ill populations

Litl 2008
Producers of next-generation computer hardware
and software for home use

Live 2000
Events management company

Lower East Side Tenement Museum 2008
New York museum that focuses on America's
urban immigrant history

Lucas Industries 1976
Manufacturer of electronic components for the
automotive and aerospace industries

Luckyfish 2007
Conveyor-belt sushi restaurant in Los Angeles

Madison Square Park 2005
Historic New York park

Magex 1998
Pioneer in the development of new
payment services

Mandarin Oriental 1985
International luxury hotels and resorts

Manhattan Records 1984
New York City based recording company

March of Dimes 1998
Organisation cofounded by Franklin D. Roosevelt in
1938 providing research, education and advocacy for
infant and childhood health

Marcus 1999
Retail outlet for luxury timepieces

M|I|C/A

Maryland Institute College of Art 2007
America's oldest accredited art school

Matter 2008
London's largest nightclub

Media Central 2001
Conglomerate of media-industry publications
and conferences

METROPOLIS

Metropolis 1999
Monthly magazine that examines contemporary
life through design and architecture

The Met
ropolitan
Opera

Metropolitan Opera 2006
America's largest classical music institution,
located in New York

MICHĒLE

Michéle 1974
Cosmetics brand for Marks and Spencer

Micro-X 1998
Range of high-performance tennis balls from Tretorn

Micrus 1997
Manufacturer of medical instruments and
medication delivery devices

MillerCoors 2008
Joint venture between brewing giants SABMiller
and Molson Coors

Modern Art Museum of Fort Worth 2002
Tadao Ando-designed museum that collects and
presents contemporary art

MOHAWK

Mohawk Fine Papers 1992
Premium paper manufacturer

The
Morgan
Library &
Museum

The Morgan Library & Museum 2006
Collection of artistic, literary and musical work
founded by J.P. Morgan in 1906

Mothercare 2004
Maternity and childcare retailer

Mozart Salzburg 2006 1998
Festival celebrating Mozart's 250th birthday

Mozart Ways 2004
International network of scholarly and historical sites
associated with the composer

Mozarthaus Vienna 2003
Museum dedicated to Mozart's life and music in the
composer's only surviving apartment

Mr. & Mrs. Aubrey Hair 1976
Personal logotype for a husband and wife

Museum für Film und Fernsehen 2006
German national film and television museum

Museum für Post und Kommunikation 1995
Museum devoted to the history of the postal service
in Germany

Museum of Arts and Design 2008
Contemporary art, craft and design museum
in New York

Museum of Contemporary Art 1990
Chicago institution dedicated to contemporary art

Museum of Contemporary Art San Diego 1992
Contemporary art museum

Museum of Glass 2002
Contemporary glass museum in Tacoma, Washington

MUSEUM OF LONDON

Museum of London 1998
Museum dedicated to the history, archaeology
and contemporary culture of London

THE MUSEUM OF THE CITY OF NEW YORK

Museum of the City of New York 1997
Presenting the history of New York City
and its people

Muzak 1998
"Audio branding" company

NapaStyle 2000
Retailer and producer of speciality food and
lifestyle products

National Botanic Garden of Wales 1997
Botanical garden situated in Carmarthenshire

National Grid 1989
Formerly the administrative body for the UK's
electricity supply, now a major international energy
utility company

NATIONAL PORTRAIT GALLERY

National Portrait Gallery 1993
The UK's national collection of historic
and contemporary portraiture

National Museums of Scotland 1998
Central administrative body responsible for seven
of Scotland's national collections

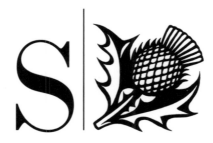

National Museums of Scotland:
Museum of Scotland 1998
Museum dedicated to the history and people
of Scotland

National Museums of Scotland:
Royal Museum 1998
Scottish museum of international artefacts

NELSON&RUSSELL
AROMATHERAPY

Nelson & Russell 2006
Aromatherapy range for Nelson's, Europe's oldest
manufacturer of homeopathic remedies

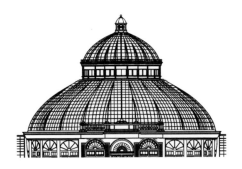

New York Botanical Garden 2004
250-acre garden and research facility featuring the
largest Victorian-era glasshouse in America

New York City Ballet 2008
America's preeminent dance company

New York City Department of Cultural Affairs 2005
Dedicated to supporting and strengthening the city's
cultural life

**New York City Economic Development
Corporation** 1992
Promotes economic growth throughout the
five boroughs

New York Jets 2001
"Gameface" graphic mascot for the NFL team

New York Magazine 2004
Revival of the original logo of the city's definitive
weekly magazine

New York Philharmonic 2008
The oldest symphony orchestra in the United States

NYPH
08

New York
Photo Festival
May 14-18

New York Photo Festival 2008
International photography festival held in New York

Next 25 2008
25th anniversary mark for one of the UK's largest
clothing retailers

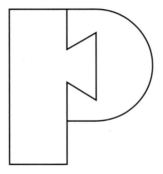

NF Purser 1962
Carpenter and joiner

92nd Street Y 2008
New York cultural and community centre

NISSAN

Nissan 1983
Automotive company

Nobrium 1971
Pharmaceuticals brand for Roche

Noguchi Museum 2004
Devoted to the life and work of the Japanese-
American sculptor Isamu Noguchi

Norton

Norton 2007
Leader in anti-virus and other computer
security software

The Oak Room

The Oak Room 2008
Iconic bar and restaurant located in New York's
Plaza Hotel

Odic Force Magazine 2007
Publication about the arts in Austin, Texas

OGLETHORPE

UNIVERSITY

Oglethorpe University 2007
Liberal arts college in Atlanta, Georgia

Ohio National Financial Services 1996
Offering financial services and solutions

The Old Kirk 1996
Residential signage for a converted church

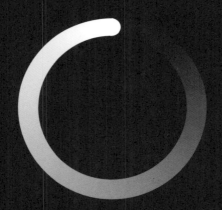

Omicron 2000
Private investment firm

1OO%design

100% Design 2007
International design trade fairs for Reed Exhibitions

One Laptop per Child 2007
Not-for-profit initiative with the goal of providing
laptop computers to children in developing nations

One&Only

One&Only Resorts 2002
Exclusive collection of international luxury resorts

Öola 1988
Candy retailer

outset.

Outset 2008
Charitable foundation supporting the visual arts

Outward Bound Center for Peacebuilding 2007
Education initiative working in regions of conflict

Oxelo 2007
Roller-sports equipment brand for the
Decathlon retail group

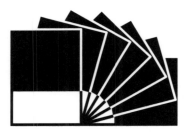

Pantone 2000
The industry-standard colour matching system

Parallax Theater 1990
Performing arts collective in Los Angeles

PathoGenesis Corporation 1992
Company researching the causes of disease

Pentagram Classic Typography Calendar 2001
Annually updated calendar showcasing classic and
contemporary typefaces

Puffin Books 2003
Penguin's imprint for children's books

Penguin Books 2003
Reworking of the iconic publishing trademark

Performing Arts Center of Greater Miami 1999
Complex of theatres and concert halls

PerryEllis

Peter Richards Productions 1991
Video producer and filmmaker

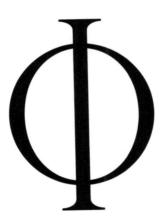

Phaidon Press 1991
Publisher of books on the visual arts

The Philadelphia Orchestra 2008
Resident orchestra at the Kimmel Center for the
Performing Arts

|||||||||| PHILHARMONIE

Philharmonie Luxembourg 2004
The national concert hall of Luxembourg

piperacity

Pipera City 2008
Retail, leisure, business and residential development
in Bucharest, Romania

Piperlime 2006
Online footware and accessories retailer owned
by the Gap

Plus 2005
International not-for-profit coalition simplifying the
management of image rights

Pont-Aven School of Contemporary Art

Pont-Aven School of Contemporary Art 2007
International fine arts institution located in the historic
artists' colony of Pont-Aven, France

Popeyes 2008
Louisiana-inspired fast food restaurant chain

Portfolio 2008
Laurence King Publishing's imprint for design study

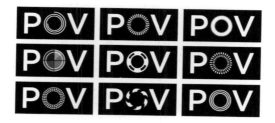

P.O.V. 2007
Award-winning documentary film series on PBS

MUSEO NACIONAL DEL **PRADO**

Museo Nacional del Prado 2003
National art museum of Spain

A Lincoln

PRESIDENT LINCOLN'S COTTAGE
AT THE SOLDIERS' HOME

President Lincoln's Cottage at the Soldiers' Home 2007
National Monument in Washington, D.C., part of the National
Trust for Historic Preservation

PRINCETON UNIVERSITY

Princeton University 2007
Ivy League university

Prior Securities 1990
Property developer

Profile Partners 2008
Media rights consultant for sporting associations,
leagues and clubs

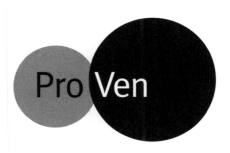

ProVen 1997
Private equity fund managers

Public Radio International 1994
American public radio network

THE PUBLIC.

The Public Theater 2008
Update of the landmark 1994 identity designed by
Pentagram for this New York performing arts institution

Quoted Companies Alliance 2000
Organisation that represents UK companies outside
the FTSE 350 Index

Radiant Lighting 1996
Distributor of Italian industrial and domestic lighting

Raymond Blanc Organics 2000
Range of organic food products created with the
renowned chef and restaurateur

RCA UVU 1991
Line of televisions from Thomson
Consumer Electronics

REBECCA HOSSACK

ART GALLERY

Rebecca Hossack Gallery 2008
Gallery of contemporary art

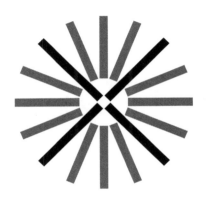

Related Experiences 2005
Entertainment, marketing and sponsorship firm

Reuters 1968
Classic wordmark for the world news service,
superceded in 1998 by a simpler mark that retained
the familiar "punched hole" motif

Catherine B. Reynolds Foundation
Program in Social Entrepreneurship 2006
New York University program that trains the next
generation of public service leaders

Rock Style 2000
Fashion exhibition at the Rock and Roll Hall of
Fame and Museum

Romeo 2008
Modern luxury hotel in Naples, Italy

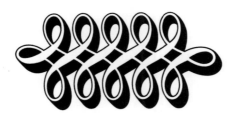

Rowe Rudd 1968
Stockbrokers

Royal College of Nursing 1984
Professional association representing nurses
throughout the UK

RIBA

Royal Institute of British Architects 2001
Professional association of UK architects

RubyTuesday

Ruby Tuesday 2007
American chain of casual dining restaurants

The Sage Gateshead 2002
Concert hall and centre for musical study

Sainsbury's Skincare 2005
Range of beauty products for a UK
supermarket chain

Saks Fifth Avenue 2007
Iconic New York retailer

Salt Lake City Public Library 2004
Library system with collections catering to all
members of the community

San Francisco 2000 1999
Not-for-profit business association

San Francisco Botanical Garden 2003
Dedicated to education and conservation

San Francisco Opera 2006
Second largest opera company in North America

San Francisco Zoo 2003
Zoo with a focus on wildlife conservation

Sandelman Partners 2006
New York-based hedge fund

SARDEGNA

SAVOY

The Savoy 2008
Pioneering luxury hotel in London

SCA 1991
Paper and wood products manufacturer

Scott Wilson 1997
Multidisciplinary design and engineering consultancy

Scottish Trade Centre 1986
Promotes Scottish industry worldwide

Scribner 1995
Simon & Schuster imprint with a distinguished
list of writers

Sekonda 2002
Watchmakers

Sequel Therapeutics 1992
Biotechnology corporation

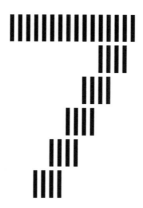

7 World Trade Center 2005
The first tower to be constructed at Ground Zero
in Lower Manhattan

7th on Sixth 1993
Seasonal fashion shows in New York

Shakespeare's Globe 1992
Historic reconstruction of Shakespeare's
original theatre

Skyscraper Museum 1997
New York museum devoted to the history
of high-rise buildings

Smith✛Nephew

Smith & Nephew 1980
Medical equipment manufacturers

Soko

Soko Aviation 2006
Private jet charter company based in Madrid

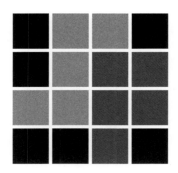

Somerset Partners 2005
Private equity firm specialising in urban
real estate investments

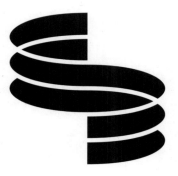

Source 2001
Imprint of Simon & Schuster publishing non-fiction

SPACE

Space.com 2000
Website focusing on space and space exploration

Spaghetti Recordings 1991
Record label founded by the Pet Shop Boys

Stanmore Implants 2008
Specialists in skeletal restructuring

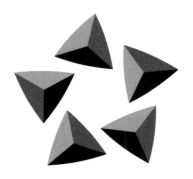

STAR ALLIANCE

Star Alliance 1996
The world's largest multinational airline alliance

stone

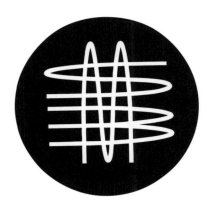

Studio of Martha Burns 1992
Designers of textiles, products and interiors

Swiss Dairy 2000
Brand of milk, juice and other dairy-related products

SYSTEM1

System One 1993
Computerised airline reservation system

T Hotel 2005
Contemporary hotel on the island of Sardinia

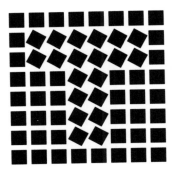

Tactics 1984
Range of high-quality men's toiletries produced
by Shiseido

Taffera Builders 2006
Homebuilders and craftsmen

Tailor Missions 2007
Christian missionary group

Telmo Rodriguez 2002
Spanish winemaker

Ad<ance

Texas A&M Advance 2007
Research magazine for Texas A&M University

Texas Biotechnology 1999
Cardiological research specialist

Thomas Hayward Auctioneers 1992
Auctioneer and appraisal company

Thomas Moran Trust 2008
Dedicated to the preservation of the artist's
Long Island studio and house

TIFFANY & CO.

Tiffany & Co. 2005
Redrawn identity for the renowned luxury retailer
founded in 1837

Time Warner Center 2004
Mixed-use office, residential and retail complex
in New York

TimesTalks 2007
Discussions between people of note and
New York Times journalists and editors

tiscali.

Tiscali 2004
Integrated internet access, portal and
e-commerce services

Tischlerei Peters 2004
Joinery and furniture-making company in Berlin

TONYFRETTONARCHITECTS

Tony Fretton Architects 2004
Contemporary architecture firm based in London

Touchstone 1999
Simon & Schuster imprint publishing political and
topical non-fiction

Le Touessrok 2007
Luxury resort in Mauritius

Tragon 2008
Marketing research and consulting firm specialising
in sensory evaluation

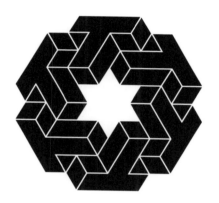

Travel Today 1989
Travel service specialising in tours to Israel

Travis Construction 1986
General contracting company

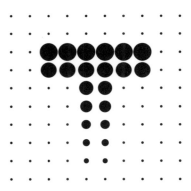

Trevi 1991
Range of premium shower fittings from
Ideal Standard

truvía

Truvia 2008
Natural no-calorie sweetener

21c Museum Hotel 2006
Contemporary art gallery and hotel in
Louisville, Kentucky

2wice

2wice 1997
Visual and performing arts magazine published
twice a year

UNITED STATES HOLOCAUST MEMORIAL MUSEUM

United States Holocaust Memorial Museum 2008
National institution for the documentation, study and
interpretation of Holocaust history and the prevention
of genocide

Uncommon Schools

EXCELLENCE ❯ NORTH ★ STAR ❮ COLLEGIATE ❯ TRUE NORTH ❮ PREPARATORY

Uncommon Schools 2006
Not-for-profit organisation that starts and manages
charter schools for low-income children

EXCELLENCE

Uncommon Schools:
Excellence Charter School 2006
New York City public school located in Brooklyn

University of California, Riverside 2006
One of the eleven campuses within the prestigious
University of California system

บทนำ

University of Michigan Museum of Art 2008
Houses one of the finest university art collections
in America

University of Surrey 1999
UK university based in Guildford

VIAGEN

Victoria and Albert Museum 1989
UK national museum of decorative arts,
design and craft

Vivantes

Vivantes 2006
Group of hospitals in Berlin

Vivo 2007
Tableware collection from porcelain company
Villeroy & Boch

VMS 2006
Software producers

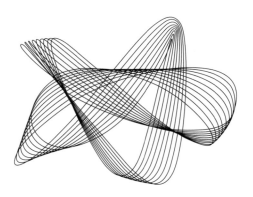

Wagamama 1997
Contemporary noodle bar chain based in the UK

Walgreens 2005
A leading drugstore chain in the United States

Waller Brothers 1979
Suppliers of office materials and accessories

Walt Disney Family Foundation 2007
Not-for-profit foundation that promotes education,
writing and scholarship about Walt Disney

The Waterways Trust 2000
Agency promoting the conservation and
regeneration of Britain's inland waterways

Webster Bank 2005
American banking corporation

Westweek 1995
Annual conference for interior designers
and architects

Wherify Wireless 2001
US location services provider

WHITNEY

Whitney Museum of American Art 2000
New York City's museum of American art,
in a famous Marcel Breuer building

Winter Capital Management 1996
International investment and advisory firm

WNYC 1981
New York's public radio station

Women's Venture Fund 2000
Provides underprivileged women with venture capital

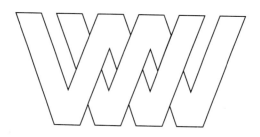

Wood & Wood 1970
Signage manufacturer

World Cup '94 1993
FIFA world championship held in the United States

World Economic Forum 1994
International not-for-profit organisation based
in Geneva, Switzerland

NY08

World
Science
Festival

World Science Festival 2008
Annual science festival held in New York

Worldwide Palliative Care Alliance 2008
A global action network that seeks to improve care
at the end of life

Xinet 2005
Network software developer

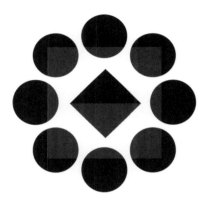

Yale School of Management 2008
Yale University's graduate school of business

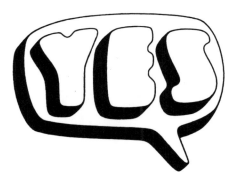

Yes 1968
Logotype designed for the cover of the prog-rock
group's eponymous first album

Young Foundation 2005
Think tank specialising in policy on social
and community issues

Zeckendorf Development 2007
Real estate development firm

Zumpano Studios 1990
Photography studio